To Read
My Words
Is To Know
My Heart

Pamela L. Goodness

To Read My Words Is To Know My Heart.
Copyright © 2021 Pamela L. Goodness.
Produced and printed
by Stillwater River Publications.
All rights reserved. Written and produced in the
United States of America. This book may not be reproduced
or sold in any form without the expressed, written
permission of the author and publisher.
Visit our website at
www.StillwaterPress.com
for more information.
First Stillwater River Publications Edition
ISBN: 978-1-955123-38-9
Library of Congress Control Number: 2021915024
1 2 3 4 5 6 7 8 9 10
Written and illustrated by Pamela L. Goodness
Published by Stillwater River Publications,
Pawtucket, RI, USA.
Publisher's Cataloging-In-Publication Data
(Prepared by The Donohue Group, Inc.)

Names: Goodness, Pamela L., author, illustrator.
Title: To read my words is to know my heart / Pamela L. Goodness.
Description: First Stillwater River Publications edition. | Pawtucket, RI, USA : Stillwater River Publications, [2021]
Identifiers: ISBN 9781955123389
Subjects: LCSH: Widowhood--Poetry. | Bereavement--Poetry. | Self-realization--Poetry. | Man-woman relationships--Poetry. | Goodness, Pamela L.--Poetry. | LCGFT: Autobiographical poetry.
Classification: LCC PS3607.O592252 T6 2021 | DDC 811/.6--dc23

The views and opinions expressed
in this book are solely those of the author
and do not necessarily reflect the views
and opinions of the publisher.

Contents

The Coming of Fall	1
Winter's Approach	2
Seasons	3
Sunshine and Seashores	4
Our Troubadour	7
Love Is	8
The Body Goes By	9
Millie	10
Menace	11
My Quarantine Life	12
Human Touch	13
Memories	17
The River	18
Forward Into Life	19
Embrace	23
The Path	24
Reaching Out Toward	25
In Your	26
Such Is	29
How Many	30
Despair	31
Your Touch	32

Why?	33
Now That You've Gone Away!	34
Triggers	35
Time	36
Who Can Say	37
Twice Broken	41
Engage	42
Your Gaze	43
Acknowledgments	45

THE COMING OF FALL

Leaves waft downward on rain swept winds,
> while darkened clouds sit low pondering their part in the threatening sky.

Darkness arrives early amid Summer's waning days
> and the fast receding sunlight casts menacing shadows of orange hues.

The stifling heat of Summer gives way to more temperate air,
> with just a hint of the cold yet to come.

Such is the fate of New England as summer fades from view.

WINTER'S APPROACH

Spiraling downward from your place in the canopy,
    your very movement a harbinger of things to
        come... chilly nights, frosty mornings, and
        lessening light.

The freedom of hot sunny days gives way to functional
    flannel and crackling fires.

The natural world retreats to a safe harbor under the now
    snow covered ground, while man stocks his larder and
    hunkers down for the long nights.

Talk to me cold winds, in your howling voice and I'll tell you of
    my yearly plight.

Of white covered mountains and sheets of ice,
    where lakes once flowed... a forbidden landscape,
    where time, for the moment, stands still.

SEASONS

Winter wains,
Spring reigns anew,
    bursting forth,
    pink clusters,
    soft breezes,
    branches shutter, raining petals down.
    Sun dappled days,
    warm rains,
Summer awaits,
    torpid days, under heated skies,
    endless light,
    bittersweet sunsets,
    moonlit sky,
Summer arrives.

SUNSHINE AND SEASHORES

As the sun moves the flowers towards its face,
> the moon moves the waves to crash against the shore.

As the sun's warmth infuses bone,
> the salted waves heal the body's ills.

As the sun's light bathes each person in joyful exaltation,
> its rays penetrate the darkness of the raging seas.

As the sun delights us with daylight and the moon lights up the night,
> so the seas offer us an endless horizon for our dreams.

OUR TROUBADOUR
(In honor of a dear friend, the late Dr. D. Russell Bailey)

He was one of us...
    broken hearted
    broken
    lost
    floundering
    bewildered
        and
    besieged with doubt and fear
        but
he sang for us... our troubadour
with courage,
    grace,
    humor.
With love
    he sang for us... our troubadour...
    now SILENT
he sings to his true love
    as they sit,
        together once more,
            on the night rainbow.

LOVE IS...

Love is... a heartbeat mirroring yours,
    ... a mind melded into one,
    ... a gentle voice offering respite,
    ... a single glance needing no words,
    ... a life singular made whole.

THE BODY GOES BY

The body goes by... wrapped in a blanket of mortality.
Regret, fear, sadness... fill the void
        and love goes unanswered.
Time stands still... then races forward.
The lover stands alone... then surrounded... then alone again.
The body goes by... life halted, joy extinguished, eternity beckons.

MILLIE

Tousled tow head, you stole my heart.
Brave defender
Small of stature… low to ground.
Scrappy… always happy.
Round pink belly… turned up for rubs.
Squinty eyes with attitude,
        jaunty gait,
              wicked waddles.
Strong of will and independent mind… you were surely
    one of a kind.
Loved you dearly,
    miss you so… on Daddy's lap you sit again.

MENACE

Trains and buses,
    Planes and cars,
        Clocks and calendars,
            Day and night.

The clocks and calendars told us when to go,
The trains, buses, planes, and cars took us where we wanted to go.
    The day told us to engage,
        the night told us to disengage.

Then, such a menace we could not see took the world we knew away.
    Will that world return one day?
        Who can say...

MY QUARANTINE LIFE

Familiar faces with welcoming smiles,
      join with comforting voices, offering cheerful hellos.
A group of singular souls once again united, share laughter
      and sorrows, gaining strength from the union.

Then the hour strikes... goodbyes and well wishes are offered.

The screen goes dark.

The door closes... I'm alone again...

The silence, like the tide, rushes in and runs back out,
      carrying with it the lightness and laughter.

The clock ticks as the minutes, once more, go slowly by.

My quarantine life begins again.

HUMAN TOUCH

A familiar smile and bright eyes, that say, "hello".
      A hand laid upon the shoulder, that says, "I understand".
           A warm embrace, that says, "I'm here for you".

These days and nights of solitude,
      the absence of human touch,
           becoming more than I can bear.

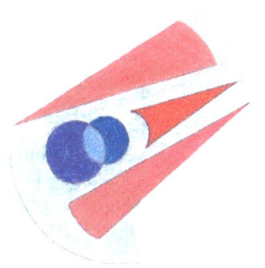

MEMORIES

Memories
    wash over ME
        then quickly drain away
            before even the first tear falls.

Memories
    overwhelm ME
        drowning, I gasp, tears flowing
            falling to my knees.

Memories
    consume ME
        with bittersweet yesterdays
            full of laughter and tears.

Memories
    pain and pleasure
        built on love
            lost forever?

THE RIVER

I see you...
      at the window you sit,
the night dark and silent.
      Outward you look,
           inward... deep in revery.
The river flows slowly by
      carrying with it the
           joys and sorrows...
                relived one last time.

FORWARD INTO LIFE

I carry you with me as I go forward into life.

You who I hold in the depths of my heart... forever loved.

A bond not put asunder by death's icy grip... forever lovers.

Treasured friendship bound not by borders
                    of time and space... forever friends.

I carry you with me as I go forward into life.

EMBRACE

Like the flower that opens as it turns toward the sun,
                the endless dark days lessen
                light finally breaks through and
My heart… guarded, quivering begins to open.

Tears that once flowed freely begin to dry,
        joy works its way through the smallest of cracks.

One who grieves as I, reaches outward from the pain
        seeking the tenderest of touch.

Embracing… the pull of life and love once more prevails.

THE PATH

Lost along the path...
      a winding path
      an unrelenting path... fraught with fear and confusion.

Lost along the path...
      a lonely path
      a dark path... fraught with guilt and sorrow.

Lost along the path... until your hand took hold of mine
      now a shining path
            ... full of promise
                  ... full of hope.

REACHING OUT TOWARD

We stood together not quite strangers, reaching out toward friends.
   We share a common journey of pain and longing,
      the road ahead a chance for laughter and joy.

You...
keen of mind,
broad of shoulder,
pleasing visage,
soulful eyes,
winsome smile... a welcoming way,
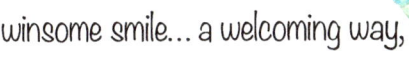
sweetness becomes you, kindness and caring as well.
   Hand in hand,
      a tender touch,
         affectionate embrace,
           impassioned kiss.
We stand together no longer strangers, reaching out toward...

IN YOUR...

In your face I see...
> dignity,
> surety,
> beauty, and courage.

In your eyes I see...
> clarity,
> soulfulness, and compassion.

In your hands I feel...
> gentleness,
> confidence,
> protection, and sensuousness.

SUCH IS...

For the joy of beginnings and all that they promise
    and the pain of endings and all the promise they take away...

Of sunshine and laughter,
    Of endless kisses and lasting embraces.
Of glances stolen and fingers entwined,
    Of secrets shared and whispered musings.
Such is... the joy of being in love
Such is... the pain of love lost
    Of tears running hot and eyes rimmed red,
Of forgotten smiles and endless ache.
    Of dreams dashed and hope rent,
Of weary days and lonely nights.

For the joy of beginnings and all that they promise
    and the pain of endings and all the promise they take away.

HOW MANY...

The heart so strong when beating for life,
      so fragile when in love.
      So please,
someone tell me...
      how many times
           can
           a
           heart be broken
           before
           it
           can no longer mend?

DESPAIR

Without warning... like a thief in the night... he came at me.
    Without armor to shield me...
        no rumors to put me on defense.

He stole the beat of my heart,
    the smile on my face,
        the glimmer of hope in my eyes,
            the skip of my step,
                the very lightness of my being.

Then he turned and walked away...
    leaving me broken in ten thousand pieces
        and
            in ten thousand ways of... DESPAIR!

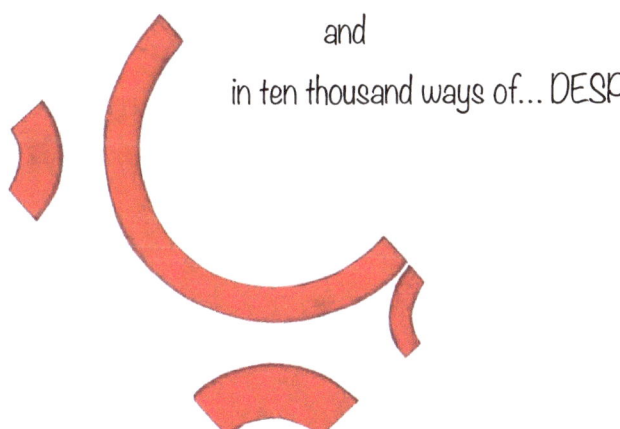

YOUR TOUCH

Your touch opened a closed heart,
    renewed in it...
      hope
      joy
        tenderness
      love

Each encounter pushed the pain further away,
    put distance between heartache and love
        then...
            you WALKED AWAY!

WHY?

The light that you ignited in my life
      when you put your hand in mine
was extinguished from my life
      when you slipped your hand from mine.
All that's left me now is the question… why?

NOW THAT YOU'VE GONE AWAY!

How strange it is that...

The Winter seems colder
and
the darkness more black.

The sun seems less bright
and
the rain more wet.

The day seems much longer
and
the night more lonely.

The tears seem hotter
and
heavier as they roll down my cheeks.

Now that you've gone away!

TRIGGERS

Triggers some call them,
       those moments when something
            or
            someone
               comes into view… that
      triggers the pain.
My triggers are the memory of you.

TIME

All that's left now
        is that familiar
                dull ache of a broken heart.

The tears still run,
        but not as often,
                and not as heavy.

My heart, weighted,
        sits in my chest,
                worn,
                      wasted.

Memories still surface
        run their course,
                then fade away.

Time is doing its work... again!

WHO CAN SAY

Who can say what turns a heart so cold
      or is so broken...
           that it cannot let love inside again.
When a love so pure, spoken with honor and grace
      is turned away... the heart breaks,
          but
     refuses to deny... the need for love,
           the healing power of love,
               the sweetness of love...
                    the pursuit of love continues.

TWICE BROKEN

Twice broken
>   the heart mends slowly again.

With trepidation and hope
>   the heart emerges slowly again

Wanting that love... so lost
>   begins the quest again.

Tenderness,
Touch,
Embrace... wanting it all again!

ENGAGE

Tentatively, I engage again.
I seek love…
> take a chance,
> be vulnerable,
> face my fears.

I seek love…
> a chance for joy,
> breathless,
> filled with hope.

YOUR GAZE

Holding your gaze elicits old fears...
rejection,
      judgement,
           betrayal,
                  disappointment,
                        pain.

Yet in your eyes I see none of those...
      but yet,
           not yet
                love either.

Will that come to be in the gaze I long to hold?

Acknowledgements

To JWH, forever in my heart...

To Steven and Dawn Porter and Emma St. Jean of Stillwater River Publishing for their continued support and their outstanding work.

About the Author
Pamela L. Goodness

A resident of Smithfield, Rhode Island. A graduate of Rhode Island College, University of Rhode Island, and Salve Regina University. A retired educator and school librarian for 24 years and now an enthusiastic volunteer at HopeHealth Hospice and Palliative Care. This second published collection of poems follows her debut work, *Walking Widowed: Reflections on a Loss.*

www.ingramcontent.com/pod-product-compliance
Lightning Source LLC
Chambersburg PA
CBHW041526090426
42736CB00035B/28